Women empowerment both working and business .

Superwoman.

business women.

Work balance
while pregnant.

By

Confidence cleantin

Women empowerment both working and business .

Cope right © CONFIDENCE CLEANTIN by 2023.

Women empowerment both working and business .

Table of content

INTRODUCTION

This award-winning book helps to Understand how to manage symptoms and maintain good health while working.

Knowing oneself, one's principles, and one's requirements

To effectively advocate for yourself, you must first comprehend who you are—your values, your needs, and your rights—in the environment in which you live and work. You must be aware of the resources that are accessible to you as well as the help that you require.

This book shows how to surround yourself with people who genuinely care about you and want what's best for you once you've come to terms with who everyone is (regardless of whose side of the family they belong to). The most important thing is that you be healthy.

Chapter 1

IMPROVED WORK-LIFE BALANCE WHILE PREGNANT

It might be difficult to achieve a better work-life balance in life, particularly when you're pregnant.
But it is undoubtedly possible to continue working and have a happy family life with careful planning and time management.

Pregnancy does not require you to give up on your goals in life or your work. Being pregnant might occasionally feel like a full-time job. When you work a full-time job, especially one that requires you to sit at a desk or smile at your clients even when you don't feel like it, this creates even more issues. But thankfully, there are strategies for dealing with the key difficulties you might experience at work while pregnant.

When should the announcement be made?

Although it is perfectly normal to be tempted to share the good news right away, it is best to wait to tell anyone until you have completed the first trimester. This is because the risk of miscarriage decreases considerably. When you do decide to share the news, make sure your boss learns about it directly from you rather than any of your coworkers.

How many common symptoms can be treated while working?

Although there are many unpleasant side effects of pregnancy, this does not permit you to take off work. Pregnancy symptoms can be managed in several ways to keep them from interfering with your career. It is possible to overcome morning sickness by eating your favorite foods (85% of pregnant women experience nausea). Healthy snacks can be consumed in little amounts to help you control your blood sugar levels and prevent nausea. If your symptoms are severe, you should talk to a doctor about the best treatments.

When should I start preparing for maternity leave?

You will need to describe the specifics of your absence before deciding to say goodbye to your place of employment for the time being. An approximate start date for your leave of absence and return date should be disclosed to your employer. You are enabling them to glimpse the end of the tunnel by providing them with a rough return date. giving a brief list of the duties for which you were accountable and giving recommendations for how your coworkers should split and handle them may be helpful.

Even though the majority of women work in fields that have no bearing on childbirth, some jobs could endanger both your health and that of your unborn child. It is crucial to speak with your doctor and get specific guidance on this.

Be truthful to yourself.

I took (too long) to realize that being pregnant came with new physical restrictions. I've always taken satisfaction in being able to do it all. I had learned to juggle a full-time career with a hectic schedule of side projects, but I didn't pull all-nighters, spend months without taking a vacation, or plan back-to-back meetings every weekday. I thought it was important to my identity to continue to present myself the same way I always did, even if I was pregnant. I was proud of that ability.

My first indication that anything needed to change was my disastrous appearance on Good Morning America. I experienced significant insomnia after I entered the third trimester, which made me irritable and forgetful. I eventually had to inform my team and manager and then reschedule my early morning meetings so I could get some rest.

According to research, women find it easier to speak out for others than for themselves, therefore I started to consult my calendar and opportunities with friends and other reliable professionals before making commitments. They would tell me not to feel bad about slowing down.

I used to have an extreme way of thinking. For instance, if a sales director at my place of employment pointed out to me that an event or webinar would help them bring in new business, I felt obligated to look into how I could make it happen right away or assumed

I had to decline them completely. Either I could give it my best or it wouldn't be worth it for me to turn up at all.

In the case of the sales director, I examine the current content calendar to determine when we might be able to add a webinar, then divide it into multiple jobs and delegate as much as I can. I've become a better manager as a result of this strategy. I used to be the first one to provide solutions when problems arose. I now invite my team members to brainstorm a few ideas on their own, which we then discuss as a group. I can better assist my team in growing and learning by taking a step back.

Audit your calendar on a weekly (or daily) basis.

The fact that my moods fluctuate day to day has been one of the most annoying things about being pregnant. Sometimes I wake up feeling relaxed and energized. On other days,

I feel drowsy and find it difficult to sit at my desk for more than a few hours due to sciatica pain that shoots through my legs and back.

I constantly review my calendar to make sure I'm taking care of myself and not forgetting anything at work. Every Sunday evening, I review my upcoming week's itinerary and mark any days that seem especially busy or demanding. When I have multiple meetings scheduled for the same day, I try to locate a couple that I can postpone until the following week, handle by email, or switch to a phone call rather than a video chat.

I'll stop and check to see if I'm putting too much strain on myself if I start to feel unwell. For instance, I would check forthcoming due dates and go over my to-do list again to see if any less urgent or critical chores might be lowered in priority. To allow myself and my team more time to breathe, I frequently can postpone internal deadlines by one or two days. If your schedule doesn't allow for this kind of flexibility, consider finding a method to take a quick break in between meetings or looking for future social gatherings you can postpone or miss.

Set three daily objectives and then extend yourself some grace.

I write down the three work-related things I intend to complete today as soon as I sit down at my computer each morning. I check that my to-do list can be completed given my schedule and physical condition. For instance, if I spend the majority of the day in meetings, one of my objectives would be to "get ready for your 1:1 at 2 PM." I also try to be as specific and grounded in reality as I can. Instead of writing "Work on the client presentation," which lacks a clear end goal, I say "Create a complete first draft of the client presentation."

I then read over the list again and think to myself, "If I finish these tasks, will I have made measurable progress toward important goals?" When the response is affirmative, I end the day with a sense of accomplishment and find it much easier to put my work aside and give myself the time I require for relaxation and refueling.

It can be difficult to say no when you're accustomed to being able to say yes. I've found that weighing the opportunity cost of accepting a new request is the best tip for honing your boundary-setting skills.

Chapter 2

The next time you're about to say yes, hold off. Think about it:

What am I going to get if I say yes?
What will I be unable to do if I do this instead?
What would be the worst scenario if I refused?
When I'm prepared to say no, I think of two sentences: one to say to the other person and one to myself. For instance, I might respond, "I'd love to, but I need to take it easier this

week," when I refuse a colleague's request. and remind me that declining at this time does not make me a bad employee. I become a tired individual as a result.

Having to overcome new constraints requires perseverance and practice. These actions have made it easier for me to extend my grace and make better investments in my health.

pregnant professionals' mental health: some things to keep in mind

Swings in mood are typical throughout pregnancy. However, if you experience anxiety or depression all the time, it may indicate a more serious issue. Pregnancy-related stress, physical changes, and regular worry can all have an impact.

Depression or anxiety can occasionally occur during pregnancy:

Depression is a prolonged period of sadness, melancholy, or irritability. Before becoming pregnant, a person may suffer from depression. However, it can also begin while a woman is pregnant for a variety of reasons, such as if she is unhappy about her pregnancy or is under a lot of stress at work or home.

Anxiety is a state of anxiety or fear about potential outcomes. Many situations during pregnancy can stress you out if you worry a lot anyway. You might be concerned that you won't make a good parent or that you won't have the money to support a child.

KidsHealth Nemours SEARCH Menu
Taking Good Care of Your Mental Health While Pregnant by Your Parents reviewed by Rupal Christine Gupta, MD, Nemours Children's Health Psychology (Behavioral Health)
Listen Print
A variety of emotions, not all of them positive, are brought on by pregnancy. You're

not the only one who worries. Worry is typical, particularly in first or unplanned pregnancies. If you're struggling with depression or anxiety, it can be even more difficult.

Take as much care of yourself as you can for the sake of your health and that of your child. Eat healthily, move your body, get enough rest, and take your prenatal vitamins.

Talk to someone if you're feeling anxious, depressed, or nervous, and know when to ask for support.
However, if you experience anxiety or depression all the time, it may indicate a more serious issue. Pregnancy-related stress, physical changes, and regular worry can all have an impact.
 Before becoming pregnant, a person may suffer from depression. However, it can also begin while a woman is pregnant for a

variety of reasons, such as if she is unhappy about her pregnancy or is under a lot of stress at work or home.

Anxiety is a state of anxiety or fear about potential outcomes. Many situations during pregnancy can stress you out if you worry a lot anyway. You might be concerned that you won't make a good parent or that you won't have the money to support a child.

Other potential problems with mental health include:

How can I get assistance?

Speak to a doctor, counselor, or therapist if you're feeling nervous or depressed, and seek treatment right away. You'll feel better faster if the treatment is started right away.

Also, discuss your general health and any previous mental health issues with your doctor. If anything arises during or after your pregnancy, your doctor needs to be aware of your entire medical history.

medication on prescription. Before starting or stopping any medications while pregnant, always see a doctor. Inform your doctor if you are pregnant or intend to get pregnant while taking any medication for a mental health condition. Unless your doctor instructs you to stop taking it, don't stop. A growing infant may experience issues from some medications, but things could get worse if you stop using them. The best course of action for you and your unborn child can be determined by your doctor.

Speech treatment. One-on-one therapy sessions with a therapist can be an excellent method to handle depression, reduce anxiety, and manage stress during pregnancy. It might also be beneficial to join a support group where you can discuss your worries with other mothers who understand what you're going through. You can deal with financial problems, the difficulty of raising a child, and other difficulties in your life by speaking with a social worker or counselor.

other strategies. Yoga, exercise, and meditation are a few hobbies that could provide you comfort. Talking to a friend, a member of your family, or a member of your religious community can help you feel better if you're feeling anxious or overwhelmed.

At some point during their pregnancy, many mothers experience anxiety or depression, and some may even require medical attention. But you and your child don't have to struggle with a mental health issue. The best course of action for both of you is to seek the assistance you require to feel better.

Social support and mental health issues during pregnancy: A connection

Social support and mental health issues during pregnancy: A connection

For women of reproductive age, being pregnant is a major occasion. It is accompanied by hormonal changes and maybe a time when mental illnesses like sadness, anxiety, and self-harm are more likely to arise. Giving the expectant mother strong social support lowers this risk and guards against complications during pregnancy and poor birth outcomes. The relationships between social support and mental illness (depression, anxiety, self-harm) in pregnant women have not, however, been thoroughly reviewed or studied in meta-analyses. To investigate the relationship between social support and mental illness (anxiety, depression, and self-harm) during pregnancy, this systematic review and meta-analysis were conducted.

to increase advocacy for maternal mental health and to exercise global leadership;

To support the integration of programs with maternal and child health initiatives, provide strategies for the promotion of psychosocial well-being, prevention, and promotion of mental disorders in mothers during pregnancy and after delivery, and provide support to the member states on evidence-based, cost-effective, and human rights several mental health and social care services in community-based settings

the mothers' mental health

According to a recent meta-analysis, 20% of new moms in poor nations have clinical depression. This is a lot higher than the salience estimates from high-income nations that were previously available. Suicide is a significant cause of death among expectant and new mothers. Although much less frequent, psychosis can still result in suicide and, in rare instances, even cause harm to the unborn child. Depression results in severe pain, impairment, and a diminished ability to meet a child's requirements. Evidence suggests that treating maternal depression decreases the risk of Your doctor should be aware of them and improves the growth and development of the newborn.

Globally, issues with maternal mental health are viewed as a significant public health challenge. Although maternal mortality continues to be the primary focus of maternal health indicators, WHO is also proposing indicators related to Healthy Life Expectancy (HLE) and Universal Health Coverage (UHC) for the Post-2015 Agenda for Development Goals. This suggests that the integrated delivery of services for mother and child health should pay more attention to mental health issues. Not only nations with great incomes are affected by the need. In low- and middle-income nations, certain academic and public health organizations have already started integrated maternal mental health programs. These have been inexpensive initiatives with the assistance of generalists or community health professionals. It has been shown that the effects extend beyond moms to include children's growth and development.

Almost all pregnant women and the first year after giving birth are susceptible to mental disorders, but certain risk factors, such as poverty, migration, extreme stress, exposure to domestic and gender-based violence, emergency and conflict situations, and low social support, tend to make certain disorders more likely to occur.

effects of postpartum maternal mental illnesses on the Mother and the Child
The mother with depression experiences severe postpartum suffering and may neglect

to adequately eat, bathe, or take care of herself in other ways.

This could make becoming sick more likely. Additionally, the risk of suicide and, although uncommon, the risk of infanticide in psychotic illnesses must be taken into account.

The general health care system, encompassing women's health, maternity, and child health care, reproductive health care, and other pertinent services, can incorporate maternal mental health.

Chapter 3

Dos and Don'ts when Working While Pregnant.

Understand how to manage symptoms and maintain good health while working.
 as well as when performing a task at work that can put the pregnancy in danger.
Maintain a fitness regimen. Energy levels can be increased by physical activity, especially for individuals who spend their days sitting at a computer. If your doctor approves, go for a

stroll after work or sign up for a prenatal exercise class.

early bedtime. Every night, try to get at least eight hours of sleep. Pillows should be positioned beneath the tummy and between the legs for increased comfort.

maintaining comfort

Everyday tasks like sitting and standing can start to feel unpleasant as the pregnancy goes on. Breaks that are brief and frequent can fight weariness. Moving around every few hours can also reduce muscle tension and stop fluid from accumulating in the feet and legs. Try these additional tactics as well:

Sitting. Long periods of sitting can be made considerably more comfortable by using an adjustable chair with strong lower back support, especially as body weight and posture vary. Use a small pillow or cushion to add additional back support for seats that aren't adjustable. To reduce swelling, elevate the legs.

Standing. Placing one foot up on a footrest, low stool, or box might be helpful for folks who must stand for extended amounts of time. Take frequent pauses and alternate your feet sometimes. Put on relaxed footwear with strong arch support. Think about donning some compression or support hose.

lifting while bending. The back can be protected by using appropriate forms, even when lifting little objects. Not at the waist, but at the knees. Lift with your legs, not your back, and keep the load close to your body. When lifting, try to avoid twisting your body.

Controlling one's stress

Workplace stress can deplete vital vitality. To reduce workplace stress:

exposure to dangerous materials

continuous standing

carrying, climbing, or heavy lifting

Unreasonable noise

High temps

Additionally, following your doctor's advice to get the recommended vaccinations will help keep you safe at home and work.

Tell your doctor if you have any concerns about any of these conditions. You and your partner can decide whether you need to take extra measures or change your job responsibilities while you are expecting.

Given that more women are joining the workforce and keeping their jobs during pregnancy, the potential effects of employment on pregnancy are a significant issue that warrants evaluation. A summary of the research examining the relationship between employment and pregnancy is provided, along with a brief historical and legal analysis. A growing body of research suggests that extended standing and long working hours may put pregnancy in danger. To improve pregnancy outcomes, doctors should advise their patients about these potential dangers and offer suggestions for early modification of occupational activities.

DEALING WITH HEAVY LABOR

Your balance may worsen during pregnancy when your center of gravity changes, increasing your risk of falling. Steer as far away from hard lifting as you can. Remember to use your legs rather than your back when getting something up from the floor. At all costs, you must avoid twisting your body.

DE-STRESSING

Utilizing to-do lists and setting priorities for important tasks will help you manage and divide your time wisely, which will help you reduce stress. Don't be afraid to ask friends, family, or coworkers for advice or just to talk things out. Yoga and meditation are wonderful practices for reducing stress and discovering inner tranquility.

Regular check-ups are crucial to have while pregnant, especially if you are working. Visit your neighborhood clinic right away for a free appointment. Pregnancy, gynecology, and fertility are the main areas of concentration at Imagination, a clinic for women's health. The clinic values respecting every client regardless of their identity, needs, wishes, choices, and beliefs and are re-outfitted with cutting-edge technology and high-quality service. Imaginative also provides early assurance in addition to pregnancy blood tests.

Know your rights when pregnant.

You might not be thinking about prejudice when you tell your coworkers about your success.

It is illegal to refuse to hire or fire a pregnant candidate if she can carry out the essential duties of the position. She cannot be denied compensation or demoted to a lower job due to her pregnancy. Furthermore, it is illegal to withhold pregnancy benefits from a woman who is not married. All of these are unlawful kinds of pregnancy discrimination.

Businesses with at least 15 employees are required to treat pregnant women equally to other job candidates or staff members with comparable skills or restrictions, according to the law.

Pregnant women's rights are safeguarded by numerous state legislatures.

It's time to let go of your fears and doubts and embrace your natural worthiness as a woman.

It's time to have a new financial conversation where you define what makes YOU happy and prosperous based on your beliefs, your financial blueprint, and your desires.

Building self-trust, confidence, and clarity around money are all steps on the path to developing a healthy relationship with money. You can empower yourself by reading this book.

In this book, you will learn:

Reset your connection with money if it has you feeling less prosperous than you should.

In the future, you'll learn how to manage money in both your work and personal life.

In your life, whether you are spending, saving, giving, or receiving it, reevaluate how you want money to manifest.

Receive the precise steps to reclaim your self-worth so you can easily and gracefully amass a high net worth.

if you've decided to lead, don't forget the value and significance of the man. It's a fulfilling and significant position that will advance your career.

What nobody tells you, though, is this

You need more than what has brought you success up to this point if you want to be a good leader. It takes effort. There are no established operational standards. Your increased level of responsibility can be intimidating.

And nobody instructs you on how to handle these situations.

Without the proper training and resources, becoming a great woman leader requires years of anxiety, dread, and uncertainty. By that time, your team is having trouble, and people are beginning to doubt you.

But becoming a great woman leader doesn't have to take years.

Leadership consultants and experts share their practical and engrossing advice in this book.

The procedures are simple and encourage you to express your unique style of leadership.

Your brand is communicated through the way you present yourself in person, via email, and on social media. As you develop your narrative, expand your network, hone your confidence, and plan your future, that brand demands careful development and crafting.

To help you identify what your brand is— who you already are, who you want to be, and how to make sure others perceive you that way—communications expert who turned her communications expertise into a multimedia brand and consultancy gives both personal and professional guidance from her lived experiences and from expert contributors.

Whether you're just starting to think about your brand or have already made the decision to reinvent yourself, this book on personal branding offers the best practices for women in business to help you engage the world, and be known and understood so you can succeed professionally, personally, and financially.

What initially began as a plain analysis of best practices has evolved into a manifesto for a new kind of power, one that is essentially female and is already manifesting itself in the workplace, in politics, and at home. It's a variation that appeals more to women (and the majority of men as well). It provides women with a roadmap for directing their professional lives, leveraging their influence for the good of others, and discovering the genuine satisfaction that comes from taking charge and influencing outcomes.

These perspectives, which draw on the authors' personal experiences, present a clear-eyed and upbeat redesign of the workplace and our familial connections, placing women in a modernized and rebuilt position of power.

And right now is the ideal time for women to assume their power. The need for a new code that focuses not only on hierarchy and having power over others but also on purpose and what power may accomplish is at risk, and what is at stake is much bigger than the next job.

The Power Code teaches you how to use the power you already possess, discover new sources of power within yourself and your community, and redesign your work and personal lives to produce less ego, more joy, and maximum impact. It serves as both a prescription for societal change and a professional handbook for individual women. All those who desire to: should read this book.

The secret is to make the most of your inherent feminine traits to draw in more clients faster and end the cycle of burnout caused by nonstop work. It's time to assess the situation, look at current management and sales strategies, and identify what is effective.

without increasing your hours of work, double your income

Create a solid sales foundation and accelerate the sales process.

Make more time, and pay attention to the important things.

Promote the value and successfully negotiate bids by acting with assurance.

This is a must-read if you're prepared to realize your full potential by utilizing your inherent skills and principles.

It is tough to scale your intuitive business if you work tirelessly all day and still can't generate enough qualified leads. The Energy Of Women: The Energy Of Your Company Business combines vigor and planning to demonstrate step-by-step how to grow a company to six figures and beyond.

Chapter 4

A groundbreaking approach to successfully navigating pregnancy at work.

The journey of pregnancy is significant.

It can be difficult to balance the need for support and the want for privacy while dealing with it while working, whether it's figuring out how to tell your boss you're expecting a baby or fitting doctor's appointments in between meetings while working even harder to prove yourself. The good news is that both environments can be successful. Your pregnant years at work will change from something you "get through" to a professional opportunity that you can embrace with confidence thanks to Carry Strong's innovative strategy. She demonstrates how to adjust to a different viewpoint, establish balance, build community, express your demands, and manage the transition from working mother to the working woman. You'll learn what job decisions to make at each stage of pregnancy, starting with the decision to become a working mother-to-be, along the way.

His astonishing account of hardship and tenacity offers fresh perspectives on the idea of achieving economic equality for all—from a prominent campaigner and fashion forerunner.

Stay away from rejection anxiety

Be on the lookout for self-discovery and loving places.

Women's Mental Health Life's Focus on Youth

Self-Care for the Body & Mind: Conditions Therapy

maternity care parenting

crisis management

WOMENS Conquering Fear

Women empowerment both working and business .

Embrace it
Verify your emotions
Find the lessons.
Recognize your worth
and possess a backup
Reduce your fear.
Face your phobia
Avoid talking badly to yourself.
Utilize your network.
Seek assistance
Takeaway
Being rejected hurts. There is no avoiding it.
Most women desire a sense of connection and belonging, especially with those they care about. It's unpleasant to feel unwelcome and unwanted by those people, whether it's for a career, a romantic relationship, or a friendship.

It's not difficult to comprehend why many WOMEN fear rejection. If it's happened to you once or more, you undoubtedly remember how painful it was and worry that it may happen again.

However, being afraid of being rejected can prevent you from taking chances and aiming high. Fortunately, with a little effort, this mindset can be changed.

A friend who disregarded a message asking to hang out was turned down for a date and refused an invitation.

a committed partner Departing for another person

Even though it never feels good when something doesn't go as planned, not all of life's experiences pan out as planned. You could feel less afraid of rejection if you remind yourself that it's just a regular part of life and everyone will experience it at some point.

It's crucial to recognize your feelings of rejection when dealing with them. If you tell yourself that you don't care if you are wounded when you do, you lose the chance to face and effectively deal with this anxiety.

After a few months, you realize that this new information has given you access to higher-paying jobs for which you were previously unqualified.

Examining what you want in a mate can help you overcome rejection worries when it comes to romantic relationships. It may also put you on the right track to locating a match right away. Educate yourself about your value

If after a few dates with someone they abruptly stop responding to texts

Ghosting is never a wise strategy, but some individuals simply have poor communication skills or believe it would be hurtful to say, "You're nice and cute, but I didn't quite feel it," while in reality, you would enjoy the candor.

You may recall that you are completely deserving of love by increasing your self-worth and confidence, which will make you feel less hesitant to continue looking for it.

Putting in writing three moments when you were most proud of yourself.

citing five examples of how you live out your ideals

reminding yourself of the benefits you may provide a spouse

Maintaining perspective

You can picture a lot of worst-case situations if you're particularly sensitive to rejection and spend a lot of time worrying about it.

Let's say you weren't accepted to your preferred graduate program. You can start to fear that you won't be accepted by any of the programs you applied to, forcing you to apply again the following year.

Chapter 5
The Fear of Aloneness and the Strength, Resilience, and Empathy it Fosters.

The Fear of Missing Out and how it encourages individualism and boundaries while pleading for self-reflection.

Social media usage is widespread. Web-based services that allow users to create public or semipublic profiles, build social networks with other users, and exchange user-generated content are considered social media.

Social media's pervasiveness in daily life is largely a result of both its socially satisfying qualities and its habit-forming features and affordances. Social media has a remarkable ability to satiate the innate need for social connection and curiosity about what others are doing. It frequently acts as a conduit for social capital by offering a wide range of information and services as well as numerous opportunities for people to connect, keep up with social events, and satisfy their need for belonging. Additionally, social media offers a consistent stream of incentives that are already built in, like alerts, notifications, likes, and "friend" requests. Through the stimulation of the brain's reward circuit and reflexive responses, these incentives act as social rewards and eventually lead to habitual media consumption [1]. As a result, checking your phone for notifications becomes a reflexive behavior that you take without thinking about it. Young people frequently display an emotional attachment to their cell phones due to the allure of social media, and many claims to feel anxious and agitated when they are removed from them.

THE brains are wired to be socially connected, and this need is as fundamental as our need for food and sex. Social media, however, also provides a platform where idealistic versions of the self are frequently selectively portrayed, providing abundant opportunities for social comparison.

The Fear of Uncertainty and how it helps us achieve our objectives and brings order to chaos.

The fear of failure and how encourages us to pay attention to warning signs and take the next best action.

The fear of endings and how it motivates people to take action heightens their respect for the lasting and reveals the beauty in regret.

The fear of losing one's freedom and how it motivates self-advocacy and leaves a lasting impact.

Self-advocacy is the capacity to persuasively advocate for oneself. This could be done to achieve favorable outcomes in any of the many situations in which you interact, including work, organizations, schools, communities, and families.

It is your right to speak out strongly about situations when decisions are being made on your behalf or that have an impact on your well-being. You are entitled to speak up for your own best interests.

But many of us don't feel confident speaking up for ourselves for various reasons. Self-advocacy is a learned behavior, but not everyone has had the chance to observe it in action or put it to use. Sometimes, the events of the past prevent us from speaking up or from believing that our demands are important enough to fight for.

You can improve your ability to speak up for yourself in an empowered manner over time.

Chapter 6

Women's important self-advocacy components.

Self-advocacy is something that everyone can learn, put into practice, and promote in others, even though it is frequently linked with persons who have specific diseases or disabilities.

The majority of self-advocacy organizations concentrate on educating adult females, particularly those with intellectual disabilities, on how to stand up and ask for the accommodations to which they are legally entitled.

But it's not always easy to understand and ask for these accommodations as an adult. There aren't many self-advocacy groups at work. Many companies are unaware of disability rights or how to make accommodations for learning problems at work, which further complicates the situation. In all honesty, these discussions and the ensuing knowledge frequently go forgotten about after high school.

Teaching students how to advocate for themselves is therefore even more crucial. Self-determination abilities are valuable outside of special schooling. Every woman can gain from having this dialogue. Self-advocacy training raises self-esteem, facilitates original problem-solving, and fosters a stronger sense of community.

Knowing oneself, one's principles, and one's requirements

To effectively advocate for yourself, you must first comprehend who you are—your values, your needs, and your rights—in the environment in which you live and work. You must be aware of the resources that are accessible to you as well as the help that you require.

To effectively advocate for yourself, you must be able to express your worth, your needs, and your human rights in a way that will be understood and provide you with the best return on your investment.

Identifying yourself requires asking the following questions:

What values do I hold?
What is most important to me, and why?
What needs do I have specifically?
What do I need to complete my tasks or take care of my obligations?
What do I require to feel valued and to keep up my physical, mental, and financial health?
What are my areas of strength and improvement?
knowing your situation

Think about it:

How can I help the team, and by extension, the entire organization?

What obligations do I have to the organization, and what obligations does the organization have to me?

Do our values and abilities align?

Can I assist the company?

Does the organization benefit from the work I do for it?

Be sensible. You might not be able to find all the fulfillment you need in one employment or one organization.

It is a great awareness to have as you decide what needs and desires this aspect of your life will fulfill. You should, at the very least, be familiar with the laws that apply to your situation, job, and/or function.

Learn about the resources that have been designated to support you both inside and outside the organization. Are there any offices set up to help you whether you're a worker, someone who requires accommodations, etc.?

Develop support

It frequently takes self-advocacy to get the adjustments that the law mandates.

All of these situations show how frequently speaking up and arguing your point is necessary to improve a situation in your life, regardless of whether it appears fair. Although there are institutional and legal structures set up to support you, it is your responsibility to speak up for the support and care you deserve. It's critical to establish a support network and to turn to it for assistance when it's needed.

bolster your network of female allies

Create a strong, open channel of communication with your manager. The best person to speak out for you is your manager. They are familiar with the business and you. Your ideal workplace ally will be knowledgeable about your requirements and the resources offered by the company, and they will guide you along the way.

Join and take the helm of groups that are set up to help you and others both inside and outside of your organization. Connect with others who share your interests and those who don't to create programs, policies, and visibility that will assist the members of your organization. Multiple perspectives and voices working together have power. There is also a plethora of knowledge to be gained from experiences.

Be someone's ally and champion. More often than not, speaking up for other women causes less anxiety than speaking up for ourselves. You'll develop more self-confidence if you speak up on behalf of others first. Those for whom you previously spoke out could turn out to be future allies.

Maintain your personal growth, social interaction (yes, the dreaded "networking"), and awareness of resources and possibilities in your area both inside and outside of your current employer. Knowing that you have options gives you strength. Occasionally, those options might be available elsewhere besides the company that is no longer meeting your needs on a personal and professional level.

When you receive a "no," take appropriate action.

Women empowerment both working and business .

You don't want abstract concepts when reading productivity articles; you want concrete methods that you can immediately do to boost your productivity. You want advice that can be used.

I did my best to fill this blog with practical advice that you may use every day of your life.
The most actionable article among them all maybe this one.

First, make a plan.

You need goals if you want to do anything. You need a plan if you wish to accomplish those objectives. a strategy to enhance. a strategy for expansion. But how do you develop that strategy? It's easy,
Write out your priorities.
Create objectives based on these priorities.
Create a plan to achieve your objectives.

Write down your priorities, objectives, and plan in one location.

Create regular rituals to consistently implement your strategy and goal.

All you need to do after creating a plan is to follow it and review it every month. Make sure you're staying on course because plans alter as your goals do.

To-do lists are useful, but how frequently do we allow them to become so crowded that we are unable to see the bottom?

It's OK. It occurs.

Thus, you must cross everything off your list

Master the Mornings

My mornings seem to be the most fruitful part of the day.

The mornings have a certain enchantment to them. If you don't think I'm telling the truth, try getting up early for 30 days. You are under no obligation to continue if it is not for you, but I am wagering that you will accept it.

Being a morning person is a fairly simple process.

Make sure you are receiving enough sleep to start, and then gradually move toward an earlier wake-up time. Begin by rising 15 minutes earlier than usual each day for a week. Once you're where you want to be, start gradually cutting back on your wake-up time by 15 minutes every few days.

To make the shift as seamless as possible, try some or all of these encouraging and fruitful ways to start your day.

Use All of Your Energy

Your energy level is the most crucial—and most overlooked—aspect of your productivity. If you lack the motivation to act, no amount of productivity advice will be of much use to you. So how can you make the most of your energy?

While getting enough sleep is crucial, sleep is not the only factor in energy. If you're feeling worn out, a short workout can be better for you than a quick snooze.

The most crucial thing is that you receive adequate sleep. Otherwise, you'll need to find additional sources of energy.

The two most effective ways to boost your energy are diet and exercise. Adopt good eating practices and gradually increase your daily workout. Your mood will improve...and the outcomes appear rather quickly.

Take Your Time Back
What happens to your time?

We all feel as though the day is too short, but why? Do you have a good sense of how your time is spent, or do you find yourself wondering where the day has gone at night? It's time to assume command, and here's how:

Cut Back on Your Commitments

Probably overcommitting yourself. We are all. You might need to use the word "no" more frequently.

The most crucial thing is to sort through your obligations and get rid of the unnecessary stuff.

Your obligations should all help you achieve your objectives. They must leave if they are not. You must focus just on the essentials if you desire margin and freedom in your life.

Narrow Your Options
Every day, you make decisions, but you might be making more than is required.

You can use the time you save by choosing a modest lifestyle to do significant things. Here are some places where you can narrow your options:

Spend less time selecting your outfit. Your wardrobe should only contain matching pieces.

Take less time choosing your meal. Divide your meals into fuel (eating the same foods repeatedly) and enjoyment (taking your time to choose). I eat the same items for breakfast and lunch, and I like dinners on special occasions.

Lessen your time spent regretting and griping. These are both completely useless. Nobody is helped by complaints, and you are injured because they cause you to think negatively. Regrets are pointless. Live, make errors, accept the lessons from them, and keep going. Form Rewarding Habits

A successful life is built on a foundation of good habits. Positive habits will lead you where you want to be, whether that involves better financial habits, reading, exercising, or whatever fits into your life.

establish a useful routine.

Want to complete a marathon but have never run before? Start by going no more than a half-mile. then gradually increase your running. Start in a way that appears almost too simple. It is so small that you can't refuse to do it.

You must exercise good habits regularly and pay close attention to them.
Even if you're "too busy," you still have time to develop healthy habits. Of course, breaking some poor habits may be necessary to make room for more positive ones, but don't stop there—replace them instead!

Establish Greater Discipline
Energy is the most crucial component of productivity, as I've previously stated, and this is true. However, even if you have energy, a lack of self-discipline might keep

you from improving and expanding. However, that's okay because you can develop your discipline.

Both in your own life and with others, discipline is contagious. Discipline feeds off of itself.

Consider establishing a new morning running schedule. You'll discover that it's simpler to maintain your other routines. It's simpler to maintain discipline in another area once you've established discipline in the first. Endorphins are released when tasks and goals are completed, and these chemicals can get you addicted to success.

Just keep in mind that a big part of discipline is learning to be gentle with yourself when you're being unruly. You can try the traditional military-style discipline if you wish, but more and more research indicates that it's preferable to be forgiving of yourself when you falter or pause for a while.

Chapter 7

Add the family in

It's simple for us to forget to bring the family along as we become preoccupied with bettering ourselves and raising our productivity.

This is essential for a happy family as well as being productive.

Helping your spouse put the new skills you acquire into practice will help you both be more productive. Use productivity tips at work, then bring them home so your family may take advantage of them.

Even your children can begin learning about productivity. The best part is that after they figure out how to be more productive, you'll be even more productive!

Many people who are employed have the dream of starting a family. However, working women and their families are particularly vulnerable during pregnancy and childbirth. Mothers who are pregnant or nursing need extra care to protect their health and the health of their babies, as well as enough time to give birth, recover, and nurse their children. Such protection guarantees a woman's equal access to the workforce as well as the maintenance of frequently essential income that is required for the welfare of her entire family.

Realizing equality of opportunity and treatment for men and women at work and enabling workers to raise children in safe environments requires ensuring the health of expecting and nursing mothers as well as safeguarding them from workplace discrimination.

Pregnancy is a joyous time for the expecting parents as well as their close and extended families. How else could it not be?

As a result, family members may go above and above to make sure the pregnancy is as easy and stress-free as possible.

There's no need to feel guilty because you're not the only one who has these ideas. Even though being pregnant is exciting, the constant offers of "help" can be overwhelming (and perhaps even a little annoying). To lessen stress, it's crucial to establish good boundaries with family members during this time.

Here are some guidelines for establishing these boundaries without alienating anyone.

Understand what you want and how to express it.

It's better to establish expectations up front and be clear about how you want to approach your pregnancy journey, just as in any other connection. Talk to your partner and put up a united front; after all, there is power in numbers.

Psychological research has shown that people react to problems more calmly and logically when they are alone rather than in a group.

 You can address issues unique to each member of the family by having individual conversations with them. Thankfully, you won't have to deal with family members who you get along with well throughout this.

Recognize that different people will have different reactions.

Every family probably has that one individual who feels the need to instruct others on how to do things. Other family members, on the other hand, may draw you to them more often because they naturally nurture and love you.

 Make it a point to surround yourself with people who genuinely care about you and want what's best for you once you've come to terms with who everyone is (regardless of whose side of the family they belong to). The most important thing is that you be healthy.

Onto your spouse, lean.

While the mother is more affected by pregnancy than the father is, it takes effort to have a safe and worry-free pregnancy. The responsibility of providing protection and acting as a filter should be assumed by partners. They ought to try to lessen the bad and increase the positive.

If you require additional emotional support during your pregnancy and afterward, Pregnancy Centers of Middle Tennessee offers peer-to-peer counseling for pregnant women.

Having stated that, allow for family member adjustments.

If you are expecting for the first time, there's a good possibility you still don't know what you want and don't want, who you want to hang out with, and who you want to avoid. It's okay if your choices change over the day or hour. Boundaries will change during the following nine months, just as moods and appetites will.

Family members will understand what you're going through, especially those who have been pregnant themselves or have been around pregnant people. Be flexible and keep the channels of communication open.

Avoid tearing down relationships.

Although you will be pregnant for nine months, family is something that lasts a lifetime. Even though you don't always feel it, realize that everything they say or do is done out of love and care for you. Long after you've given birth, the ability to pick your battles will be useful to you.

While your family will respect your wishes during this time, they might insist on pitching in in some way. This could involve cooking, cleaning, watching older kids, or even providing transportation to your appointments. You will eventually acknowledge that you do require assistance. Make a list of your to-do list that includes tasks that family members can assist you with. By keeping them involved, you'll not only be able to do much more but also make them happy.

Pregnancy causes a lot of physical and emotional changes in expectant mothers. Your feet are bloated, and your back hurts. At the sight of chocolate bars, you start crying. These days, even your belly button looks different! However, if your partner is there with you throughout the entire process, keep in mind that the pregnancy isn't just about you.

It's crucial to support someone during their pregnancy, labor, and early parenting. Whether you are the expectant mother's partner, the baby's father, or you are helping a single mother-to-be, you play a critical position in making sure she receives the support she needs throughout this life-altering period.

An emotional rollercoaster, pregnancy can feel like the longest nine months of some women's life. Relationships may suffer as a result of the strain of new parenthood. For the sake of the mother, the infant, and your relationship, it's crucial to assist in meeting the new mother's physical and mental health needs.

Mental health

Be aware of how hormone changes can cause mood swings. If your partner is feeling sick, she may occasionally cry or become dissatisfied with being pregnant.

Getting ready for childbirth

Attending antenatal classes with your partner and reading books on pregnancy and newborns are also helpful ways to get ready for the baby's arrival. If you can, attend your prenatal appointments, especially the more crucial ones like scans, so you can see how the pregnancy is developing firsthand.

Adapting to being a parent

After the baby is born, your family's way of life will change. During this frequently emotional time, it's important to take care of your baby, yourself, and your relationship.

Your partner will get some rest and you will both benefit from spending time with your newborn alone.

Make time for play by conversing with your child, singing, making silly expressions, or funny noises. All of these things aid in developing the infant's communication abilities from a young age.

Especially if she underwent a cesarean delivery, there may be things your spouse cannot do while she is recovering from childbirth. Be aware of her limits and offer all assistance you can.

Being able to breastfeed can be challenging for some new mothers, so if your partner is having problems, offer support. While she is eating, she could experience pain or even anxiety. Each feeding may take a while, but there may be times when you can give your baby a bottle of extracted milk instead. This can help you strengthen your relationship with your infant and give your partner a break. But not everyone will like this. For some women, expressing milk hurts and can be uncomfortable. Wait a few weeks if your partner chooses to express so the infant can become accustomed to breastfeeding before introducing a bottle.

Chapter 8

Managing the exhaustion and discomfort of pregnancy at work.

You should be aware of your rights to maternity leave, antenatal care, and benefits if you are working while pregnant.

Speak to your physician, midwife, or occupational health nurse if you have any concerns regarding your health while working.

You can also speak with a representative from your union, your employer, or human resources (HR) at your place of employment.

When you inform your employer that you are expecting, they should work with you to do a risk assessment to determine whether your position offers any dangers to you or your unborn child.

They must take reasonable steps to eliminate such hazards if there are any. This may entail adjusting your work schedule.

It can be illegal for you to continue working if you do work that involves chemicals, lead, X-rays, or a lot of lifting.

In this situation, your employer is required to provide you with an alternate position on the same terms and circumstances as your prior employment.

Your company should suspend you with full pay (or grant you paid leave) for however long it takes to avoid the risk if there is no safe alternative.

You're likely to feel warmer than usual when pregnant. Hormonal changes and an increase in blood flow to the skin are to blame for this.

If you are working while pregnant, you should be aware of your rights to maternity leave, antenatal care, and benefits.

If you have any worries about your health while working, consult a doctor, midwife, or occupational health nurse.

Additionally, you have the option of speaking with a union, employer, or human resources (HR) representative at your place of employment.

When you tell your employer you are pregnant, they ought to collaborate with you to conduct a risk analysis to see if your job poses any threats to you or your unborn child.

If there are any such risks, they must take reasonable measures to eliminate them. This could require changing your work routine.

If you perform work that involves chemicals, lead, X-rays, or a lot of lifting, it may be prohibited for you to continue working.

In this case, your company must offer you a different position with the same benefits and restrictions as your old employment.

If there is no safe alternative, your employer should suspend you with full pay (or provide you with paid leave) for however long it takes to eliminate the risk.

When pregnant, you might feel warmer than usual. This is caused by hormonal changes and an increase in blood flow to the skin. Furthermore, you probably sweat more. You could assist by

Natural fibers should be worn loosely since they are more absorbent and breathable than synthetic ones.

Use an electric fan to keep your room cool to make the temperature more pleasant. To feel more refreshed, wash often.

consume plenty of water

being exhausted

Feeling worn out or even fatigued is typical throughout pregnancy, especially during the first 12 weeks or so. The already nauseating effects of morning sickness might be made worse by fatigue. Although being exhausted won't harm you or your unborn child, it can make life feel more difficult, particularly in the beginning before you've told anyone about your pregnancy.

The extra weight you are carrying can cause you to feel tired later on in your pregnancy.

As your baby gets older, it may become more difficult to get a good night's sleep. You can find it uncomfortable if you choose to lie down, or you might have to get up to use the restroom just as you start to feel comfortable.

Your sleep patterns may vary during pregnancy, and you might wake up more often at night and get less restorative sleep.
The only way to deal with it is to try to get as much sleep as you can. Accept any help that coworkers or family members may offer, and schedule some downtime during the day to unwind.